UPDOG

IN THE SPOTLIGHT

ARIANA GRANDE

POP VOCAL POWERHOUSE

Rachel Rose

Lerner Publications ◆ Minneapolis

Lerner Publications Company
An imprint of Lerner Publishing Group, Inc.
241 First Avenue North
Minneapolis, MN 55401 USA

For reading levels and more information, look up this title at www.lernerbooks.com.

Main body text set in ITC Franklin Gothic Std.
Typeface provided by Adobe Systems.

Editor: Angel Kidd **Photo Editor:** Angel Kidd

Library of Congress Cataloging-in-Publication Data

Names: Rose, Rachel, 1968– author.
Title: Ariana Grande : pop vocal powerhouse / Rachel Rose.
Description: Minneapolis : Lerner Publications, 2025. | Series: In the spotlight (Updog books) | Includes bibliographical references and index. | Audience: Ages 8–11 | Audience: Grades 2–3
Identifiers: LCCN 2024037290 (print) | LCCN 2024037291 (ebook) | ISBN 9798765669167 (library binding) | ISBN 9798765684474 (paperback) | ISBN 9798765679012 (epub)
Subjects: LCSH: Grande, Ariana—Juvenile literature. | Singers—United States—Biography—Juvenile literature. | LCGFT: Biographies.
Classification: LCC ML3930.G724 R67 2025 (print) | LCC ML3930.G724 (ebook) | DDC 782.42164092 [B]—dc23/eng/20240819

LC record available at https://lccn.loc.gov/2024037290
LC ebook record available at https://lccn.loc.gov/2024037291

Manufactured in the United States of America
1-1011536-53887-9/25/2024

TABLE OF CONTENTS

An Early Start 4

Road to Stardom 10

Star Stats 16

All-Around Star 20

Just like Ariana Grande 29

Glossary 30

Check It Out! 31

Index 32

An Early Start

Ariana Grande sang her heart out.

She was performing at the 2024 Met Gala.

As a child, Ariana loved to act and sing.

She was in school plays
and local theater.

At fifteen, Ariana starred in a Broadway musical called *13*.

She won a National Youth Theatre Association Award.

UP NEXT!

Big break.

Road to Stardom

Grande was on the TV show *Victorious*.

She played Cat Valentine.

Grande wrote the song "Put Your Hearts Up" for her *Victorious* fans.

She went on to do another TV show called *Sam & Cat*.

But Grande's heart
wasn't in the new show.

She wanted to spend more time writing songs and singing.

STAR STATS

Full name: Ariana Grande-Butera

Date of birth: June 26, 1993

Hometown: Los Angeles, California

HONORS

Grande hit number one on the *Billboard* 200 chart with her first album, *Yours Truly.*

She won Artist of the Year at the 2016 American Music Awards.

Grande also won two Grammy Awards.

In 2013, Grande released her first album, *Yours Truly*.

She sang with rapper Mac Miller on the album's song "The Way."

UP NEXT!

Many talents.

All-Around Star

Grande made many popular albums.

She toured around the world and sang with other big celebrities.

Grande started her own makeup and beauty line called r.e.m. beauty.

She also gives back by donating to charities.

Grande is a role model. She speaks about loving your body.

She also talks about mental health issues.

In 2024, Grande came out with her seventh album.

She also returned to her acting roots. She starred in the movie *Wicked*.

A lot more still lies ahead for this great superstar!

Just like Ariana Grande

Grande used her many talents to follow her dreams. What talents do you have? Is there something you can do to help make one of your dreams come true?

GLOSSARY

celebrity: a famous person

donate: to give money or time to help a charity or other group

mental health: a person's emotional and mental well-being

perform: to entertain an audience

role model: someone to look up to

CHECK IT OUT!

Biography: Ariana Grande
https://www.biography.com/musicians/ariana-grande

Britannica Kids: Ariana Grande
https://kids.britannica.com/students/article/Ariana-Grande/631762

Kiddle: Ariana Grande Facts for Kids
https://kids.kiddle.co/Ariana_Grande

Rains, Dalton. *Pop Music*. Mendota Heights, MN: Focus Readers, 2025.

Rose, Rachel. *BLACKPINK: K-Pop Sensations*. Minneapolis: Lerner Publications, 2026.

Schwartz, Heather E. *Ariana Grande: Music Superstar*. Minneapolis: Lerner Publications, 2021.

INDEX

album, 17–20, 26

Broadway, 8

Grammy Awards, 17

Miller, Mac, 19

Sam & Cat, 13

Victorious, 10, 12

Wicked, 27

PHOTO ACKNOWLEDGMENTS

Image credits: Kevin Mazur/MG24/Getty Images, pp. 4–5, 26; Lester Cohen/Getty Images, p. 6; Bruce Glikas/Getty Images, pp. 7, 18; Jim Spellman/Getty Images, p. 8; Walter McBride/Getty Images, p. 9; Noel Vasquez/Getty Images, p. 10; Micah Smith/Getty Images, p. 11; Dario Cantatore/Getty Images, p. 12; Ben A. Pruchnie/Getty Images, p. 13; Troy Rizzo/Getty Images, p. 14; Gilbert Carrasquillo/Getty Images, p. 15; AP Photo/Media Punch/INSTARimages, p. 16; Chelsea Lauren/Getty Images, p. 19; Robino Salvatore/Getty Images, p. 20; Jason LaVeris/Getty Images, p. 21; Cindy Ord/Getty Images, p. 22; Dave Hogan/Getty Images, p. 23; David Becker/Getty Images, p. 24; Paul Morigi/Getty Images, p. 25; Matthew Stockman/Getty Images, p. 27; AP Photo/Evan Agostini/Invision, p. 28. Design elements: oxygen/Getty Images; Medesulda/Getty Images.

Cover image: AP Photo/Media Punch/INSTARimages.